READING POWER

American Tycoons

Cornelius Vanderbilt

and the Railroad Industry

Lewis K. Parker

The Rosen Publishing Group's
PowerKids Press™
New York

Published in 2003 by The Rosen Publishing Group, Inc.
29 East 21st Street, New York, NY 10010

First Edition

Book Design: Daniel Hosek

Library of Congress Cataloging-in-Publication Data

Parker, Lewis K.
Cornelius Vanderbilt and the railroad industry / Lewis K. Parker.
       p. cm. — (American tycoons)
Summary: A short biography of Cornelius Vanderbilt, the steamship and railroad tycoon, focusing on his success as a business man.
Includes bibliographical references and index.
ISBN 0-8239-6450-7 (library binding)
1. Vanderbilt, Cornelius, 1794-1877. 2. Businessmen—United States—Biography—Juvenile literature. 3. Railroads—United States—History—Juvenile literature. [1. Vanderbilt, Cornelius, 1794-1877. 2. Businesspeople. 3. Railroads.] I. Title.
CT275.V23 P37 2003
385'.092—dc21

                                        2002001799

Contents

Cornelius Vanderbilt

Cornelius Vanderbilt was a very hard worker. Vanderbilt's work with steamboats and the railroad industry made him one of the richest American tycoons ever.

Cornelius Vanderbilt was born on May 27, 1794, in Staten Island, New York.

Vanderbilt's birthplace in Staten Island

Cornelius Vanderbilt

The Ferry Business

When he was sixteen years old, Vanderbilt borrowed $100 from his mother. He bought a small sailboat to use as a ferry. For 18 cents a trip, he carried people and goods between New York City and Staten Island. Vanderbilt quickly became successful and bought more boats.

> "I didn't feel as much real satisfaction when I made two million [dollars]…as I did on that bright May morning…when I stepped into my own [boat]."
> —Cornelius Vanderbilt

Staten Island in 1777

Check It Out

In one year, Vanderbilt was able to pay back his mother the money he borrowed.

In 1813, Cornelius Vanderbilt married Sophia Johnson. They had thirteen children—four sons and nine daughters. Sophia Vanderbilt was also successful in business. She ran a hotel and restaurant that Vanderbilt bought in New Jersey. The restaurant was known for its good food and service.

Cornelius Vanderbilt and Sophia Johnson (above) were married on December 19, 1813.

The Steamboat Business

Around this time, people started using steamboats to travel. They were much faster than sailboats. In 1818, Vanderbilt sold his sailboats and started working for Thomas Gibbons. Gibbons owned a steamboat and ran a ferry business between New York and New Jersey. Vanderbilt helped Gibbons's steamboat business grow.

Steamboats were often used as ferries in New York City's harbor.

11

In 1829, Vanderbilt bought one of Gibbons's steamboats and started his own steamboat business. By 1834, Vanderbilt owned more than 1,000 steamboats. He made a lot of money by charging riders less than other ferry companies. This made other companies go out of business. Vanderbilt bought some of these companies. Other companies even paid Vanderbilt not to have a steamboat ferry route near theirs.

People called Vanderbilt "Commodore" because so much of his work was with boats.

Vanderbilt used this large steamboat to travel on the ocean.

Check It Out

Vanderbilt received $40,000 a month from one company in return for not having a route near it.

Working on the Railroad

After the Civil War started, Vanderbilt sold his steamboat business. Vanderbilt thought that railroads were going to be more useful than steamboats. Soon, he controlled two railroad companies around New York City. By 1867, Vanderbilt was in control of the New York Central Railroad. It was the second largest railroad in the United States.

Vanderbilt was about seventy years old when he started his railroad business.

Railroads were used to move people and goods.

15

Vanderbilt improved the railroads that he controlled. He used new steel rails in place of old, rusty iron rails. On his railroad line that went from Buffalo, New York, to Albany, New York, Vanderbilt added another set of tracks. Vanderbilt's improvements allowed him to use larger trains, which could carry more people and freight. Vanderbilt made millions of dollars from his railroad business.

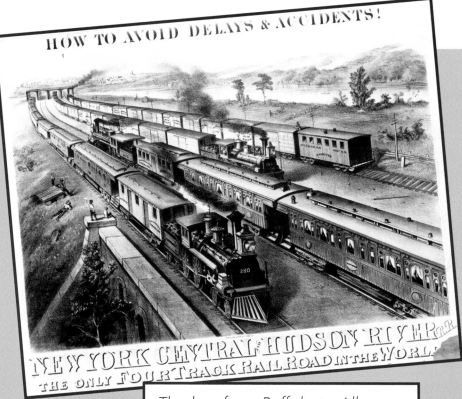

The line from Buffalo to Albany was the only railroad line in the world to have four sets of tracks.

Vanderbilt improved the insides of his trains so people could travel in comfort.

"I have been insane on the subject of moneymaking all my life."
—Cornelius Vanderbilt

Cornelius Vanderbilt worked with his son, William, to make his railroad business grow. In 1873, the New York Central Railroad became the first railroad that ran from New York to Chicago.

After Cornelius Vanderbilt died, his son, William, took over the railroad business.

Grand Central Depot

Check It Out

Between 1869 and 1871, Vanderbilt built Grand Central Depot in New York City. At the time, it was the largest train station in the world.

After Vanderbilt

Vanderbilt died on January 4, 1877, in New York City. He had about $105 million, which is worth more than $96 billion today. When he died, Vanderbilt had more people working for him than any other business in the United States. Today, people still use the railroads that Cornelius Vanderbilt started more than 100 years ago.

Time Line

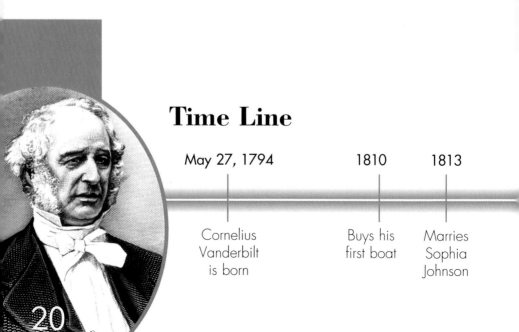

May 27, 1794	1810	1813
Cornelius Vanderbilt is born	Buys his first boat	Marries Sophia Johnson

Check It Out

Vanderbilt did not give money to many charities. His biggest gift was $1 million to Central University in Tennessee. It was later named Vanderbilt University.

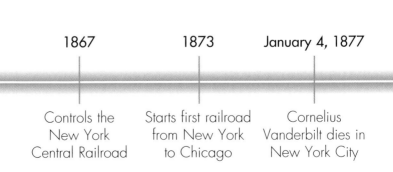

1867	1873	January 4, 1877
Controls the New York Central Railroad	Starts first railroad from New York to Chicago	Cornelius Vanderbilt dies in New York City

Glossary

charities (**char**-uh-teez) groups that raise money for people in need

Civil War (**sihv**-uhl **wor**) the war fought from 1861 to 1865 between the southern and northern parts of the United States

commodore (**kah**-muh-dor) a captain in the navy

depot (**dee**-poh) a bus or railroad station

ferry (**fehr**-ee) a boat that regularly carries people and goods across a body of water

freight (**frayt**) goods that are carried on boats, trains, or airplanes

industry (**ihn**-duh-stree) a kind of business that makes a particular product, usually in a factory

route (**root**) a path of travel

steamboat (**steem**-boht) a boat that is driven by steam

tycoons (ty-**koonz**) businesspeople with a lot of money and power

university (yoo-nuh-**ver**-suh-tee) a school where people go after high school

Resources

Books

American Tycoons
by Carl Green
Enslow Publishers (1999)

The Rise of Industry 1860–1900
by Christopher Collier and James Lincoln Collier
Benchmark Books (2000)

Web Sites

Due to the changing nature of Internet links, PowerKids Press has developed an online list of Web sites related to the subjects of this book. This site is updated regularly. Please use this link to access the list:

http://www.powerkidslinks.com/aty/cvr/

Index

C

Civil War, 14

F

ferry, 6
ferry business, 11
ferry companies, 12
freight, 16

G

Gibbons, Thomas, 11–12

I

industry, 4

N

New York Central
 Railroad, 14, 18, 21

R

railroad, 14–16, 18, 20–21
route, 12–13

S

steamboat, 4, 11–14

T

tycoons, 4

Word Count: 527

Note to Librarians, Teachers, and Parents

If reading is a challenge, Reading Power is a solution! Reading Power is perfect for readers who want high-interest subject matter at an accessible reading level. These fact-filled, photo-illustrated books are designed for readers who want straightforward vocabulary, engaging topics, and a manageable reading experience. With clear picture/text correspondence, leveled Reading Power books put the reader in charge. Now readers have the power to get the information they want and the skills they need in a user-friendly format.